MORE PRAISE FOR

TOMMY PICO

"Funny and honest and wickedly clever."

—SHERMAN ALEXIE

"Pico is a poet of canny instincts, his lyric is somehow so casual and so so serious at the same time. He is determined to blow your mind apart, and . . . you should let him."

—ALEXANDER CHEE

"Mix of hey that's poetry (uncanny resistance) with hey that's a text and smashing goals & fulfilling them along the way & saying my parents fulfilled them. Doing it differently being alive & an artist. I love this work. Unpredictable & sweet & strong to continue."

—EILEEN MYLES

"The self-conscious labor of these poems explores a culture of asides, stutters, stammers, and media glitches. It's no wonder Tommy Pico manages to name and claim identity while also reminding us of his (and our!) limitlessness."

—JERICHO BROWN

"A poet who will not hesitate calling out winter as a death threat from nature, Tommy Pico hears the wild frequencies in the mountains and rivers of cities. The marriage of extraordinary sharp writing with the most astute commentary on almost every possible thing a human will feel, think, do, dance like, or smell like."

—CACONRAD

"On the narrowing frontier between song & speech, memory & oblivion, future & no future, Native & American, *IRL* is Heraclitan, a river of text and sweat, whipping worlds into the silence of white pages: a new masterpiece. And a new kind of masterpiece. It's a lyric epic of desire whose hero renounces heroism."

—ARIANA REINES

"A gleeful combination of exuberance and threat."

—SIMONE WHITE

"Pico centers his second book-length poem on the trap of conforming to identity stereotypes as he ponders his reluctance to write about nature as a Native American . . . In making the subliminal overt, Pico reclaims power by calling out microaggressions and drawing attention to himself in the face of oppression."

—PUBLISHERS WEEKLY, Starred Review

"[*Nature Poem*] finds Pico incorporating or indirectly referencing his surroundings in freewheeling, intimate verse, while turning a humorous lens on life as a queer man."

—OUT MAGAZINE

"Humor lays the groundwork for a hard truth and, for poet Tommy Pico, that hard truth is about living as an indigenous person in occupied America. . . . Pico's poetry builds a contemporary Native American persona, one that occupies multiple spaces simultaneously: New York City, the internet, pop music, and Grindr. It's an identity that's determined to be heard by the culture at large."

***—THE ORGANIST*/KCRW**

"Instead of following the conventions of the pastoral tradition, in which nature is revered, Pico adopts a tragicomic view. On the one hand, the land of his native people can be described with great reverence, desert nights that 'chill and sparkle and swoon with metal/ lighting up the dark universe.' On the other, that same landscape carries and extends legacies of racism and genocide that Pico is determined not to forget."

—THE SAN FRANCISCO CHRONICLE

"Pico has pulled me out of a poetry slump. His poems make me want to live with more poetry, to read, write, and revel in poetry as a form that does not have to be a container."

—BROOKLYN MAGAZINE

"Few people capture New York, queerness, and the artful use of hashtags in a poem quite like Tommy Pico."

—NYLON

Published by Tin House Books, Portland, Oregon, and Brooklyn, New York

Distributed by W. W. Norton & Company

Library of Congress Cataloging-in-Publication Data

Names: Pico, Tommy, author.
Title: Junk / by Tommy Pico.
Description: First U.S. edition. | Portland, Oregon : Tin House Books, 2018.
Identifiers: LCCN 2018002485| ISBN 9781941040973 (paperback) |
ISBN 9781941040980 (ebook)
Classification: LCC PS3616.I288 J86 2018 | DDC 811/.6—dc23
LC record available at https://lccn.loc.gov/2018002485

First US Edition 2018
Printed in the USA
Interior design by Jakob Vala

www.tinhouse.com

Tin House Books
Portland, Oregon & Brooklyn, New York

Frenching with a mouthful of M&M's dunno if I feel polluted
or into it—the lights go low across the multiplex Temple of

canoodling and Junk food A collision of corn dog bites and
chunky salsa to achieve a spiritual escape velocity Why am I in

this cup holder? *B/c yr bubbly, dummy* But I feel squeeze cheese
uneasy In Faggotland coupling is at best delicate precarious &

rarefied Eggshells At worst, a snipe hunt Love in the time of
climate change Should I be nervous? No, it's too dark in here

for that There's light and a screen & our moon faces, reflecting
This is an epic, dummy Get yr muse Hail Janet Jackson, patron

saint of Eternal Utility but Selective Relevance I whisper *Feed-
back, feedback* into the bedding Usually when you gag it's bc

something needs to come *out* So it strikes me as funny ha ha
funny to gag while trying to stuff someone's whole Junk *in*

Everything that can cross I am crossing: eyes arms shoulders
Back to bed, come back here The air is heavy feathers in mid-

summer, literally and metaphorically in my foul apt above the
chicken slaughterhouse where we wheeze awake Yr bangs look

real perf n coiffed n strangely I smell like horror burgers n you
smell like lavender doves and all the best stuff Yr comforting,

like getting fucked on an empty stomach Funny but a lil obvious
like a wrecking ball factory going out of business I feel held up,

like yr examining my x-rays and nothing's broken I'm like why
does this meaty yuppie man want me to wake up in his arms

but Janet says *leave yr worries behind* I'm trying to close my
eyes I'm trying to close my eyes I'm tryin to close my Shudder

yr forehead against mine tectonic San Andreas in the West
Village karaoke piano gay bar whatever I still can't close my

eyes I just spent $13 dollars on this margarita Black Velvet is
loud and extra theater kid in the world around us This is where

you come to lose yrself and This is where I feel extra jagged
Junk not immediately useful but I'm still someone I can't stop

lookin at ppl's Junk generally so u can imagine how hard it is
at the gym I try to keep eye contact but yr orbs soft n breath-

less glow their orblight all over me—we're seeing subarctic
farming in Alaska for the first time Green in the hazel country:

that's what I'd call the color of yr eyes Squeeze an hour before
my weekend in Philly just to chill n make out wink-wink and

get yelled at by a jerk squad cruising past us in a royal blue rust
bucket in Queens n thinkin about you brings a rush of warmth

like a stiff drink Settles over my rocky butte Interest sparked
like a neon pink band sweatshirt A tabby-fat heart I'm a brick

in stadium lights like so fantastically broken but I'm gummy-
peachy keen Junk gets a bad rap because capitalism Junk isn't

garbage It's not outlived its purpose—Junk awaits its next life
Google *viral* vs *bacterial*, then try to sleep I had a tweet once

called "Netflix & Pills" that went sort of viral and you said you
were in a viral video dancing on a patio with a group of gay

norms (of course) on Fire Island (of course) in a thong (of
course) and it made me want to punch a pigeon Ppl buck like

fuck when they feel their self-esteem is under siege Shame is
isolating I write "very specific baths" What kind of grey scrutiny

do you cast into the mirror? And if being pinned down by light,
the squirming My roommate found an unused juicer at his job

Two story thrift store between a methadone clinic and wild
mushroom truffle oil chicken tikka masala pizza In common

thrift store parlance, black leather vegans—as in the verb *to
become vegan*—if it's a gift My first question is "can you put ice

cream in that and still call it juice?" I unzip yr pants with my
teeth in the denim jacket afternoon and I'm as surprised as you

Hoover maneuvers The benefit of sober knob-slobbing Bottom
lip only bleeds a little bit and it's hard to imagine zippers do

much else but reveal yr Junk Cookie dough brownie vanilla
frozen yogurt swirl wipe Whenever we finish n I stare directly

at you, you act like I spilled something Jump up as if to get a
paper towel and hang in the kitchen evading my peepers Is this

what you'd call "Hart Crane-ing" Is saying "goose flesh" instead
of "goose bumps" evil incarnate Is it wrong 2 call yr partner a

mirror in the sense that when we're together I'm with myself
in a way I can't escape A train whistles in the distance I court

containment An octopus hugged in a box but you say being seen
is a prison We're buffering pretty hard all over each other I am

face 2 face with the perfectly tweezed eyebrows of anxiety You
can't curate yrself with abandon Read: to look at carefully The

covers up to our shoulders we lie in the couchbed of our
preconceptions, separating I steady walk back to the land

where I dunno u Took you long fuckin enough Now I'm stupid
and sugar-free and frothing The only thing harder than writing

is quitting candy And the only thing harder than quitting candy
is walking all day and buttering into bed in my body Now that

I'm fully inhabiting my cement maybe I'm closer to the sacral
joy of thinking into my ribcage? Convention says a book shd be

this long but I'm only interested in writing as long as you want
to read in one sitting My aura is a strawberry shortcake dessert

bar and the popular American corn snack Funyuns My safe
word is *Go to hell Katy Perry* pronounced "Catty" I'm writing a

sitcom about butts and counting called *Number Two* The tag-
line is "turn the other cheek" Most times I'm a maniac, other

times losing an arm wrestling match Sitting for longer and
longer but paying less and less attention, evolutionarily Is a

load easier to swallow with a "we" *We've known for centuries
that time is a bossy bird curdler* Protrude from the green and

calling it "bud" Sometimes you need to read something more
than once My co-pilot is Mary Jane The theme is harmony of

a gradient Let's hold hands and walk to the water taxi in
matching tank tops but we call the tank tops "wedges" and the

wedges are a Chipwich and our Cherry Cokes are a summer
afternoon where we can't do anything but lean into the grass

at that carousel park in Dumbo with the lap of the river and
the dollhouse of lower Manhattan face-fucking us while we

neck and, later, face-fuck The days are burnt packets of fake
sugar in Faggotland and Sundays are the blurry worst I'm

takin notes in therapy like "be more in the moment" Everyone,
they say, is trying to quiet the buzz but here in the white waves

in the ring of yr absence I chafe to chatter Leap into a scream
of swans rubbing their swan cocks against the water's ass

Starving Junk in the sticky soda of my boy meat Spit on that
rock hard narrative make it glisten fuck oh fuck My head a

rabid Sega frantic 16-bit divination My hands huge Venn
diagrams: the middle is where I miss you filling me Honey, in

the raw It's odd to feel someone slip away drilling their Junk
inside you The sky is still and shy and surfing News Flash—

Predictions are insecure but here r the rainbow road's possible
paths: Cum delta Choke my loneliness daddy More graphics

more resolution more jagged chin cliffs more anarchist sex
dolls more jewel teeth more tears on the pizza more hungry

boy somewhere in the noise machine The fat Junk wags against
my throat Junk is charming in the hallows Dude leans into me

like cigs half asleep *you know how some ppl are workaholics
Well I'm an alcoholic* Today's jaw lick click clocks sops the

syrup leaking from my mores I mean pores One more time
plz can I ride plz just one more time I have the tightest pink-

est purse Sorry *clutch* Let's play a game called sociopath, or
gay man Let's bottomless brunch Let's Let's Let's petal bagel

w/ strawberry tofu cream cheese toasted snickerdoodle
smoothie fuchsia purée adrenaline hole bellinis I'll eat it daddy

baby I'm the opposite of a foodie I'm like a junkie Don't blame
the Junk for being discarded Hey do you do you remember in

the free-from-winter but not-quite-spring after poet's brunch
with Molly Amy Chelsea and Sarah Jean we went traipsing thru

slushy Williamsburg and wound up at that store Junk where u
bought all those old matchbooks for a "living room conversation

piece" I grabbed a June Jordan near the door as we entered the
labyrinth and read random gripping lines while you lifted dusty

old china wiry broken radios n hopeful cassettes We got to the
counter you took the book from me tossed it with the matches

and said "my treat" Well I told u I'd write it into something I am
in the Junk shop of my 30s A weird thing happens when u enter:

nothing You look up to a sea of button ups and cuffed jeans and
casual pomade flip-dos Objectively, my father is a tribal chair-

man and I'm his speech writer I started one on the back of a bill
for therapy where Dr. John tells me Go with the first glass pearl

or arrowhead or whatever Says I can't be wrong I like to read
poems one at a time Word for word at first Try to strip them

and see their bones before, eventually dressing them in my
clothes Smellin of my orange Hermes toilet water and then

BOOM June Jordan reminds me to call my mother Receive the
beached bottle Crash it against some pop rocks So dizzy I swear

to god I'd smash my face against the mirror if I wasn't on my
way to Shake Shack again OK so then finally I write my version

of the poem Replacing the unimportant gods w/ peanut butter
cookies and "Apollo" with "Shake Shack" or "fracking" which

my mom says caused another earthquake in Oklahoma n nearly
reaches the end of her sentence b4 breaking into the chorus

from "New York, New York" Apollo is just a cracked statue &
we're moving on to the wildfires in Indonesia Bobby Flay's

rum punch Whoever thought up heaven must also think we're
really gullible These days no one can stand up in a movie

theater w/o me thinkin it's all over White men open fire My
brain is a kiddie pool filled with pinwheels & Oreo dust Ppl are

too busy callin themselves "poets" to notice the canary died I
have only ever gotten better at being my color, w/ the banded

lines and the tremors and the blues The smell of pumpkin pie
cooling Chomping thru a whole baked brie wheel *We go deep*

& we don't get no sleep Everyone is reading *The Life-Changing*
Magic of Tidying Up—basically an anti-junk manifesto but it

has a point You should be accountable to what you touch The
sound of Styrofoam rubbing on Styrofoam Is it possible to

manifest desire I mean to consider yrself fly as fuck without
another's recognition Touch all this Junk Are hands made for

anything but touchin yr body, is a ponder for almost every
Janet jam Consumed with being "acceptable" *Dummy, that's*

never been in yr vocabulary Yr thinking of "exceptional," duh It's
cool, they sound similar The older I get the more people move

to the city turn 26 fascinated by the *wacky* G train *Holy shit,*
the birthday boy just puked The JMZ grinds its wheel teeth

behind you Embarrassment is so scalding sometimes in a
February freeze I remember the night you vomited on me after

we'd made out just to warm up Self-hatred is a sweltering
disease not cured by living in the pathogens at a mustache

party The chunks dribble down yr glued-on Fu Manchu There
is a kind of waltz to being that drunk But I'm getting into hero

territory Everything new is just something to forget unless you
still have the mustache to prove it San Loco's "surprisingly

addictive" sangria Terracotta breaking The engine of capital-
ism: dope, dicks, misc bullshit Junk is its accumulation Not as

indistinct as "thing" not as dramatic as "trash" It's important
to value the Junk, Junk has the best stories *Custard* is like the

most disgusting word I thought the point of seeing each other
was to see each other How is being seen by me a bad thing?

Dudes shd talk less generally and def talk less about music Yr
reputation recedes you I call it aggressive mediocrity "Comfort"

food is a perky euphemism "Oblivion" food may be a touch too
negs Why aren't more things horchata I can't see exactly where

the binder clips begin and the half used Best Buy gift cards end
Is it that sight is possessive? The way "to see" is also to

apprehend? It can't be that sight is isolating It's like taking a dip
With the water on all ends you are suddenly your whole entire

skin The only thing funner than a Junk shop is wig shopping
Wigs are possibly the only thing I'd find suspect at the Junk

shop It's hard to trust an old wig Day 17: I found freshwater
and food The water was in a fountain at the gym The food was

in a protein shake container, also at the gym Sadness makes me
punchy, but I'm a lover A boy w/ the clear skin of a plant-based

diet and whose sharp edges put the pro in protein has started
saying *what's up* to me in the locker room I've always wondered

why ppl use religion to justify their prejudices cos shouldn't yr
religion be challenging you to undo them? And then I meet gym

ppl and I'm like *eyeroll* Maybe religion *is* just a place where ppl
fortify their fears I look at him then look at me in disbelief He's

like the morning and I'm like crud underneath a toenail My
stupid waterbed body Shame is such a shutdown sucking feta

from an olive's soul *Oh he def has an edible butt* says someone
out of the void which means some butts are edible and some

butts are inedible Incredible Do I have an edible butt Edible
butt Edible butt That's pardon the expression bullshit Edible is

the birthright of all butts I hate gay guys so much There's this
idea that only some bodies are worthy of desire and the others

don't even exist And from the guts of my anger, this glowing I
dunno I've stopped counting the days The anger snowdrifts So

many ways of seeing that reveal and when the anger gets
replaced by empathy and I *feel* you, it's almost sad—letting go

of our hazel country The impotence of Junk Birthday cake
scented candle The bartender getting too drunk on 5 dollar

margarita cheeseburger happy hour Sirens call attention
toward tragedy Land is the trauma of lava The islands

squeezing from the deep Fall came quick Beirut Baghdad Paris
Mizzou Yemen Turkey Niger Calais Allepo Egypt Chicago

Indonesia Radiation from Fukushima is in fact all over the
Pacific Open carry men show up at protests An Arab guy in

Astoria beaten in his bodega by white ppl tellin him *Go Home*
Milk-toned Oregon militias bellow *Give us back our land* in the

most unironic ways Does America's shirt look eggshell-white
or more like white-panic? The problem with pizza is it keeps

getting eaten The J train is stalled and another part of Brooklyn
is on fire Sirens dry rub the brittle morning In 2011 I lived in

the 11th arr. In a month I was finally able to order a pig shaped
princess cake in nearly coherent French AND correct Euro at

the boulangerie with yellow frosting curtains and the picnic
heat The firm lady at the counter, who for weeks spied me

silently point at the croissants and raspberry tarts and chicken
baguette n fling whatever coins, gave me a lil wink I suaved

home victorious First Kumeyaay in Paris with my little pink
treat Junk loves reflection Two buskers sang "Hey, Joe" on Canal

St. Martin n waved me over to sip 1664s and neck Our wobbly
night at the firefighter's ball betting which ones would wink

back and giggle bubbles into our weak vodka crans Today
municipal workers scrub blood off those streets Refresh.

Refresh. Refresh. Still you didn't like the pic Roy posted of me
reading at the Whitney in my purple tee and acid washed

spray-on skinnies rolled to perfect *wtf is wrong with you*
spectacle What critics have called my gem-like ankles Stupid

blustery shame Winter windchill at memorializing the saboteur
No dummy, you have to go with yrself Commit I'm an expert at

peacing out We all have our survival strategies growing up on
the rez America's first POW camps In a way I'm indebted to

dissociation Shouting gets so small it's almost quaint I fold it
into my pocket Even now it's hard for me to come/back to my

body It's here I hold all my selves all my Junk, and if everything
that passes through the pile changes the pile: You have changed

me The sentiment, cut loose from shame, floats free in the
crescent evening Wd you call laughing at a dog heartily licking

his balls "Dog-tainment"? Junk is discovery *and* anchor A chair
is a chair is a footstool is a prop is a metaphor is a directive

(have a seat) is kindling *No dummy, "discovery" is too colonial*
If I have to defend keeping Janet Jackson in a poem, the devil is

truly a peanut (gallery) I'm not judgmental I just don't like any-
thing you do Who cares what *I* think? Run thru life convinced

yr all neutrality n earnest curiosity but that's a lie Judgment
happens, but that's not a ship-falling-off-the-edge-of-the-world

situation See momentum The thrust The wave The object and
its continuation The lilt at the end of a breath Movement at the

end of an obstruction Growth in the breakage, usually when
talking to yrself in the shower or singing a Janet Stupid fragile

male ego I whisper *feedback, feedback* into the pillow I dream
and in my dream I am leaving New York for Philly This dream

happens approx every time I sign a rent check Philly sure likes
to brandish its colonial history Maybe I'm just bitter some ppl

get to have history But for reals on some streets they keep the
charming, archaic whale blubber burning oil lamp fixtures

which, no longer using oil, might seem obsolete Whose structure points at a function we might no longer "get" I've never lit

a lamp myself "Knowing" changes with age Ppl give you credit
to appreciate the junk Nod to a past you'd like to remember So

I will always keep Janet Miss Jackson If Yr Nasty in the poem If
anything exists in 50 years I have faith in the future's ability to

Google Ask Jeeves Yahoo Answers YouTube tutorial Webinar
whatever Try to freehand an ampersand Ppl say Diogenes and

King James and shit and I accommodate yr idea of Ages Will
you make space for mine I imagine you saying "lecithin" Teeth

digging into yr tongue and frankly, it makes me sick Reach into
the pile Feel the skin on the inside of yr worship It's like yr

asking me to tell you, as I rove over the broom handles and
the keychains and the half bottle of vermouth—Yes of course

it's all good, Yr Junk in any season Yr Junk in any city Yr Junk in
any element I'm guilty of treating my man like my enemy As if

he stole something from me that I have to bicker back But in
the argument's zenith I'm petty af I don't want to be petty I

want to be petted as in give me a cat but here we are—*Dummy,
you'll always succumb to yourself* Shame like an Energizer

battery it keeps going, and going, and going It's juvenile to
think you can glide thru life perfectly undisturbed I know what

it's like to feel as if every confrontation will end with someone
literally dead To dodge confrontation instead Atoms re-

arrange and remake, like proteins or Legos A tuna melt is best
on pressed bread splashed w/ butter n garnished with curly

fries Everyone, they say, has a new pop punk fuck boy built like
a yeti with the stick straight Veronica Lake bang Dating is hard

bc gay men are a garbage fire Why do ppl say they "love food"
like it's a revelation A secret *I'm such a food-aholic* Oh, like

literally every other living organism in existence? Junk
breathes How dare ppl be born in the '90s I like tall guys bc I'm

lookin for someone who can fend off the ppl who will kill us
when we swap spit in the karaoke booth That time we hung

out with our giddy newness at the Mexican restaurant by the
bookstore with the best reading series in the city and the

glassy eyes zooming in on each other Seeing only the wonder,
like canary yellow on a canary or when our sky wraps up in

Earth's shadow This is my yellow heart This is my gauzy two-
people-gazing-across-the-night-into-each-other instrumental

situation Who owns the attraction passing between bodies We
say neurons "fire" because a frame of mind needs the border of

poetry Something fuzzy buzzing Your face glows coastal, leaves
me feelin fine as the powdery shoreline at low tide *Dummy, all*

our lives we are the wavelengths of light who escape the negative
space Urge toward sunset scattered roadways, morning haze,

and the gusting forward of time Oh shut the fuck up Voices
change How dare you tether me to lines I wrote in like 2009

Goin over yr Junky poems huh? Do you ever wish you cd just be
always one self? "Whole" is a privilege and a pedestal Whole

Foods has a delicious hot buffet Red alert DEFCON 5 Deep Space
9 lol Clack, clack of expensive shoes slapping down the train

platform A car backfiring Sputter of gunfire on a Snapchat story
I don't know where the feeling is or what to do with it n spent

most of the day in bed with my eyes squeezed shut but then
we went to the park and ate a vanilla ice cream sandwich and

an empanada We went to the vigil n marched n held hands Got
pizza and played pool at a gay bar with John & Peter bc what-

ever season it is it will not be open season on my spirit And
then went to karaoke and after, I said *I love you* for the first

time in my life said it to someone I'm dating and you said *I love you so much* and I know where that feeling is and what to do

with it It's going all over the place How are the people most fucked by society treated the absolute worst, and those most

coddled given the most opportunity How can "happiness" be anything more than a metaphor for privilege Thus my

obsession with punchlines—stop me if you've heard this one: *Who will save your stole?* This is a thot experiment and there I

go drooling When you nurse a crush for two years you become a boss at being tipsy All that rub, no climax *Let's wait awhile*

before we go too far I thot falling in love was a burden A kind of crowding on my landscape *Love creates space, dummy Doesn't*

take it up Tangy harpsichord Crunching into a crisp pink lady The sherbet swirls on these apples is maybe the most perfect

color in nature The perfect denim jacket is worn, rolled, and the color of heavy fog tumbling from the Pacific into the bay

"Love" is a soft fur trim The way old cotton wears thin on broad shoulders A line of tiny buttons on a pair of purple wool

gloves With its fats and its salts and its sugars, Junk food was designed *not* to satisfy I have a crush on this thrift store clerk

whose curly hair bowls when he belly lols I don't actually know
what that means, "perfect denim jacket" Just what I'd feel if I

had it Trash is thrashy but Junk is gunk I sat on another pair of
glasses and cried for a legit 15 minutes but the lenses can be

recut and put into new frames I have a drawer of Junk glasses
missing an arm or a lens *It could be worth something one day*

I suppose Junk is also a way of not letting go—containing the
stasis We cd potentially be alive our whole life How to be Junk

and decisive I have this way of saying "bus" so that it rhymes
with "moose" when I want to be festive As in *Gtg or I'm gonna*

miss my boose I claw for reasons to live lol and find them Some
days you just have to take the boose to Crown Heights for a

tune-up Junk is anti-stasis Ashes to atoms In the sense that
Junk wants to become again How the fuck do ppl still have

energy for sweaty sexytimes after midnight He wants to go
again and I want to go home, have an indica chamomile and

slack like a boss It's sad, not havin a 20's stamina but once I
learned you can make someone cum three times a night and

they can still dump u I was like *Welp* Trapped there, I don't
want to eat apples from the tree in the yard in the neighbor-

hood of that feeling anymore I like mood/lighting and draw a
bath in my brain The bubbles spread across my knees like relief

Do you hear cicadas? Crinkle cuts & queso with bacon and
jalapeño The movie starts n then a bump in the Internet con-

nection *We are now boarding rows 15 and higher* Suitcase cpl
of months A couch surfing budget Eat Pray (Prey?) Love cpl

of months All over the motherfucking planet looking good
while I'm at it What I want changes like an accent, elusive as a

mantra said with different inflections Go home with a dude cos
he lives in a condo w/ a foam bed bc who wants to spend

another night on Oakland friend's green oval shag again
Traveling broke is truly a younger person's game Look into

the dark sky and think, *how far out does it go?* Voices exist as
thick rubber planets in my throat hole I'm a goddamn catch

Molasses, or Mole Asses Day-Glo pink bell sleeves Over a life,
the first times pile like dirty sheets And suddenly I'm living a

season with the alcoholic San Francisco cos he was wearin a
red bandanna in his profile pic We've all done it A thunderstorm

rush under covers and subsequent clinic visit Basement nasal
twee bands & their delicate white fallings feelings If his tight

grey slacks are high-wasted and I'm high/wasted and he sits
arms crossed in the karaoke spot and the huge bulge and

widening pre cum stain, I will, in fact, genuflect Best thing abt
leaving town is the poem suddenly comes differently—as if it

needs a kind of obscurity in order to really be seen Hindsight,
for example Sight becomes a craft of memory Memory—the

fantasy that actually happened I believe in butterscotch candy
and chocolate covered gummy bears from the pic n mix at the

Virgin Atlantic terminal in San Francisco Int'l Sun smooched
n sparkling famous band afternoon Unfurling atop East River

State Park Kalamata olive pot Jolly Ranchers n falafel balls
The sky in its gown of nostalgia For a minute we were in the

donut I mean moment Confessed a mutual love of scratching
the paint off things Melty like cheese like whipped cream Cake

batter double fried disco lights Bobbing like those inflatable
tube dudes Continually recycling excitement Feedback Fizzy

All I've ever wanted was to feel the heat with somebody But
mostly affairs r sort of short/intense like gas Worst thing abt

this famous artist cokehead cheating on his girlfriend w/ me is
the shameful thrall Pitching a tent in this terrain Let's talk abt

how Uranus tilted Abt how glass is neither solid nor liquid It's
always moving The lake in the winter when the ppl traverse

the surface in spiky crampons Which is not a portmanteau So
obsessed with warm in the winter Warmth is the anomaly

Something that requires generation Engines in the stars In the
cores Seeking heat Most of the universe burns cold Not havin

a bf in so long I forgot how something as mundane as holding
hands makes a target of us You reach yr arm out to rest on my

shoulders and I pull away I'm not afraid of intimacy I'm scared
of assault I want 2 love in spite of the violence *Black cat 9 lives*

short days long nights livin on the edge not afraid to die Iraq
facing the possibility of total economic collapse on the back of

war and falling oil prices vs Australia's avocado shortage One
food truck in Sydney has resorted to using frozen stuffs Gasp!

Café calamities It's not even theater Sympathies swell along
familiar lines Focus instead on dry skin and yr steadily expan-

ding waistline Impulse aisle induced psychosis Too much
credit is ascribed the panic of "self-control" It's like some

choices formed before I was born Hard work is hard but
decisions, like metaphors, are built within a moat of desire

Love in a hopeless kingdom Like, okay sugar and booze feel
good, then bad Sometimes real bad But art feels bad before it

feels even worse And then even the best n I just want to wear a
pretty dress When I left yr house for the last time you said "aw,

now *I'm* sad" Grief is another way of making it all about *you*
How costume is yr grief? How girthy? How banshee? Everyone

wants to be loud and public and right Whose grief can piss the
farthest Is the poem distinct or another kind of feed I'm starvin

Hope for yr Junk Reinvention Innovation Buttercream Words
compound meaning all the time BEER ME yells a man at the

bar n suddenly *to beer*—converted to verb Make a beer of me
Like Junk passing 2 garbage passing 2 ashes passing 2 atoms

Extinction wipes words from earth *The only way to fight ISIS
is to wipe them from the face of the earth* But I'm from a group

that others have tried to wipe from the face of the earth Had
reasons like yours—savages, bloodthirsty, inhuman—War

doesn't work Anything simple is a ruse Life somehow earns its
complications Never just the night in question I'm not saying

gay men are bad I'm just saying I don't like them They keep
saying they "are paleo now, bitch" L'Oréal True Grip textur-

izing powder hair Pubes trimmed like a French garden (if any
at all) Rag & Bone combat boots treading every social inter-

action like a battle My skin mite as well be camouflage-colored
to these homonormative Hollister cologne smelling mean ass

eyerolling trollers Which is why I was so freaked you even
asked me out in the first place It's embarrassing, to discover

under the scar tissue Under the finding love and worth in
yrself Under the rejection of normative approval STILL an

ember for the threat of "validation" Junk is chunky n indistinct
until Zoom zoom zoom Summer nights rubbing yr Junk like

trying to start a fire Trying to reignite us Liftoff! But you had
too much Bulleit bang bang Can you call it dry humping if we

were in the waves in front of Caracas non penetration Yr
relationship with my ass: You can't keep yr hands off it Give it

a little tap when I get up to use the bathroom at this mid-
western restaurant we stumble into on my frigid birthday

Myriad sour beers we try but don't like Slide yr hand into my
back pocket at the record store yew dragged me to bc *vinyl is*

really the only way to hear Diana And even tho I've omg duh
heard all her songs I snap on the big headphones & pretend

anything can happen You bite it softly and moan *fuck oh yeah oh my god* I don't really get it I do those lunges with the hand

weights and concentrate on my ass when walkin upstairs but nothing inflates It's COOL I'll never have one of those majestic,

rock-climbing asses jutting from a small arch threatening to peak over a waistband I'll never have a David ass I don't get

that Just have to focus on other things But yr so... into it So into it that *oh hey, there's my ass again* lookin behind my

shoulder in the mirror Moisturize twice a day Buy it plush red pillows Give my*self* a little tap in the morning before coffee A

spring as we grab our scarves hats gloves boots sweaters jackets Head out the door in2 this frigid thing ppl in the northeast

dare to call a day Yr not even an "ass man" Yew just dig mine One of the reasons I hate gay men is it's allllllll about capital

"d" Dick and capital "b" Booty Here's another one: Blow jobs on rooftops, rims on the riverfront, wet sauna handies like

panning for gold What's the big deal There's nothing surprising abt getting off Getting off is like, *why are you so obsessed with*

me? Let's talk after you've finished off Yr head is clearly fogged up in cum shots Junk unused is but a dream, the You of the

future I dreamed up a cargo ship full of multicolored storage
units It didn't capsize like in the movies It just floated there,

exposing its anatomy And woke up a full 30 secs before the
sadness kicked in Do you ever wish you were always sleeping

I'm a basic butterfingers when it comes to affection, it keeps
slipping out of my paws It doesn't belong to me or any1 None

of the feels do, they just move through It's odd, to suddenly
lose containment—the guts busting Where to start collecting

or recollecting Thousands of people blockade the Sejm in
Warsaw over media restrictions I used to practice holding my

breath in biology class in high school One minute, then two,
then three Just to prove the clock moved The seconds tick into

lunch It's fun, like a trick who resembles neon Mostly, body
feels like a duty A stiff Spurting ketchup bottle Find a joy in the

drum of yr breath Let's not even talk about how Junk mail is
basically keeping the post office alive rn Another seven offers

to restructure my debt in Spanish Exclamation mark envelopes
Pink stationary urges urgency Bolded words to pressure and

confer ACT NOW New York will have you stomping thru a slow
couple on the sidewalk even when you have no real place to go

Huffingly annoyed at the small line at the pharmacy in the
Duane Reade Train delayed on the Brooklyn Bridge The city,

it seems, was made to fray patience To pump my blood
pressure I want a Snickers n a pack of Peeps n to never go to a

gay bachelor party Doesn't a bachelor party suggest ho-ing's
last hurrah? And if both grooms attend? I'm on a scavenger

hunt for the point I have my looking glass Okay so it gives you
the excuse to eat a stripper's ass at a Airbnb in Chinatown in

front of all yr friends March strobe-like to a karaoke booth
alone at 2PM in Queens bc TGI-Saturday Those damn cicadas

won't shut the fuck up Oasis or ocean, the much 2 much We
swap spit in the karaoke booth An attendant comes in tells us

to stop How many peeps try to bump uglies in private karaoke,
like is there a secret queer history of the private booth *Yr*

thinkin too much, dummy Close yr eyes Abstain from that flat
grey jaded-feeling Here comes failure He wears white Being

butt-fucked is a symbolic encounter with death *Omg dummy,*
you need to smoke less Is it called a bruise when the lips are

marbled by sudden heavy hickeys in the space between new
strangers Texts I recite to friends who avalanche *aww, he's a*

keeper "Feelings r neither created nor destroyed but conserve over time" is the only logical conclusion to dating in the city

The hook up/break up ratio Fucking in the bathroom at the pie place infuses you with apple cinnamon sage encrusted

chicken pot We don't say "boysenberry" enough, as a species Feedback has no intention, it reflects the proximity of output

to input The buzz, The buzz screaming, The buzz screaming at its screams The echo chamber of internet social media Choose

yr own disaster *Dummy, where are you going with this?* I watch TV @ the gym It's quaint, a real live TV-set like back in the day

War War War on every station on every show Syria Turkey Nigeria France Chicago Colorado Springs White men open fire

on protesters White man opens fire at clinic White Man Opens Fire White Man Opens Fire *Terrorists are waging war on our*

way of life the pundits say Well imagine growing up on a rez, bud Do you smell the oranges on my fingertips? Do you hear

the cicadas? Writing is witness—in ink the revelation stays My therapist says *um, what?* My bank says *overdraft fee* My bffs

are plethora My health has its hand on its hip, looking mighty impatient I accidentally type BOOL instead of BOOK n suddenly

I'm writing a BOOL It's hard to date someone with no sense of
play but probs harder to date someone who won't stop I'm

sorry I turn everything into a punchline—the grief is loud, but
laffs are louder I feel something dark pulling me down, as sure

as I feel the ancestors yanking me up I will stop writing abt the
conflict of my body when it goes away Consequently I can never

sleep—It's too dark in there Junk is scary bc this cd be the end,
sang into a megaphone and the megaphone is a BBQ joint *I've*

struck a chord you say, leaving the table Pulled pork is my
favorite *Who the hell eats a sandwich with a knife and fork?!*

Every fight is composed mostly of *not* the night in question
What I meant to say was *I'm not yr dad, dick* Well what *I* meant

to say was *I'm not the kids who made fun of you for having*
tortillas at lunch, dummy You are the kind of person who keeps

a white shirt white I am literally guac stains A snip across our
class difference I tried being fancy once, with the white shorts

but then I sat in orange Fanta on the train *Dummy, you should*
have called a car Some Junk will ultimately be garbage The pin

from the boutonniere you slid onto my sweater the night we
first met *Let me know what you like if you like I'll go down*

d-down down down d-down down Junk is waiting for a decision
like last call Grandma's steel 12 string The silver cuff from that

shop in Old Town How much of yr past lingers, having left Like
my grandfather, I keep eagles Who believes in spiritual horse-

shit? There is a common misconception abt NDN ppl, namely
everything but esp the sads One blistery summer the pepper

tree rotted, black/twisted licorice crawling up the ground of
my grandma's garden A reminder Grandpa was not my

grandpa by blood Bikini Kill had an album called *Reject All
American* Not as good as *The C.D. Version of the First Two

Records or *Pussy Whipped* but yielded "R.I.P." Ppl die Some-
times a song reminds me abt pink peppers There is something

essentially American abt me The way I grip the yellow pole in
the U-Bahn The way I sit with my thimble of coffee at Point

Éphémère The way I water red gardenias in the front yard
(despite bourbon & liberal arts) There's a common mis-

conception abt NDNs, namely everything, but esp when pink
pepper trees grow like cages in the valley Eagle screams sky-

ward and He's in a graveyard & I'm not there Grief is like Junk
in the sense that it's complicated *Just say it, dummy* Today I'm

grieving Paris I like that song "Super Rich Kids" by Frank Ocean
It has a similar plank plank plank plank to "Bennie & the Jets" I

lived in another country I had abandon More James Baldwin
than Ernest Hemingway Fearless exploring denied

Kumeyaays for all of recorded history It means something
ancestral when you've been penned in for generations I didn't

believe the sun could set at 10PM Fearless is wrong Not fear
conquered but fear seen, lived alongside *That's* what felt

attacked that night Dadaab refugee camp in the middle of a
Kenyan desert Syrian refugees can't work legally in Turkey

Lebanon outright refuses to erect camps for fear refugees will
want to stay Denmark passes a law so border agents can legally

seize valuables & cash from asylum seekers Suspicion is feelin
w/o proof, a strong belief, a knowing based on previous knowl-

edge w/o knotty newness Ask me what it's like to live in a camp
on yr own land for three hundred years Feel bereft by winter-

time But really, the cold is all around us Warmth is the luxury
Junk as insulation from the cold/shoulder of people Junk as a

way of being at the center of yr own universe Engine of old
strobe lights that smell like tar when turned on A site for old

technology, like poetic forms Should we talk abt boats? Fuck
obligation *Content* as it applies to creative effort and *Brand*

is it applies to identity are the most disgusting words in human
history Raillan says *beginnings* Wilkinson, *on the other hand—*

Nalini says *Milli Vanilli* or *Nilla Wafers were my father's faves*
"I feel you I feel you," I keep saying—back carved into a loaf of

back carved twice will twist the spine and make one leg shorter
One barrel of a chest Confusing body movements that smooth

when the diaphragm's in heavy use "I feel you I feel you" I keep
saying, which means: constant pain and paying attention "I feel

you" I keep saying amid a burst of incoherent language, lang-
uage bein the thing that we pour, molten n cool and use and

chip and melt down n I dunno what to say when my date
blabs *reading is boring* That he'd never finished a book b4 bc

words don't *grab* him/his attention I wanted to say "attention
is a resource, the groundwater Condensation The band of

elemental scar tissue protects us from solar wind Like a joint
passed back and forth until it singes our lips—You gotta grab

each other" But that's some hero shit Maybe reading *is* boring?
Does everything have to be climactic? So terror tallies shorter

and shorter, so Jacob says or was it Mason? Maybe the names
are more like Chunky n Young Bird, Chuka, Limpy n them and

I say "and them" and mean how in "the sticks" where I lived
The rez The mailboxes were like maypoles at the end of the

earth I mean beginning of the dirt road that leads to the home
that is no longer there, but I rest my cheek against the cool

linoleum of my memory when Canal Street is too thick or the
subway slams into the two men fighting in front of me and how

generally, Limpy n them and Beebee and Angel and Turtle and
Sterling n them and Chop n them Someone wd drive home and

say *who's that at the mailbox* You would suck your teeth and
say *Bee Sting n them* and you generally don't want to be one of

them, but if needed, if someone was messin with you at school
They n them burned with intimidation Thems wd literally fight

all yr battles for you The whir of yr coffeemaker The squeal of
yr springs announce our interlocking In this story the well was

full (of love, ew) The hero cd come and go as he pleased Every1
thinks they're unprecedented Without a replenishing source

of groundwater, the well depleted lil by lil and the only bucket
he had was a hat (jk gross) So he got trapped down there A

lock on the bridge An old self I pat on the head Post yr grief
Have a personal anecdote It's crass, performative, self-centered,

and only cute when I do it Call out everyone's lack of grieving
everything simultaneously Just because I'm not in public

mourning doesn't mean I'm not w/ grief Mourning sickness
First things first: get out of bed Another black man shot by

police Another missing woman in Indian country Another trans
person discovered by the roadside Another mass shooting They

pile like stones and overtake the poem Resist wanting to burn it
all down Native basket grasses paperwhites mint and irises

elderberry and honeysuckle A bunch of baby oak trees and
pines The yucca The butterfly bush Somehow ppl still can't

read my mind The pearl, peck-heavy man at the gym with the
penis I call "hosey" needles me into the showers Curiosity with-

out danger—Or maybe desire informed by danger I can't exist
that way in my body I live too much in danger's pocket My kink

is minding my own business But the poem is much more hos-
pitable Embrace the pivot & plow What's the point of living

like a beautiful shut-in I'll stop writing abt my body's danger
when one of those goes away *I'm game if you still are* But you

aren't, as if our feeling was a heat and we just stepped into a
windy February night—slapped from love *I'm emptier when*

we're together It's never just the night in question *They always*
come back I tell Chantal *They always have* Which isn't true, but

satisfaction lies in the delivery Pizza I sweat thru my shirt,
buying my coffee in dimes n quarters or when the checkout

person swipes my debit card at the end of the month and it
says *Processing* . . . On the old couch in the tower the flood sings:

You are small and cold and here for so little, you are already
gone I'm not like a regular slut, I'm like a fun slut Thoughts

jamming jagged and panicked into the next The wreckage at
least suggests reflection—Now what? It's never just the night

in question Memory echoes *Come on dummy, you can't re-*
member everything Roy and I argue side-eyed abt how we met

Junk is so anti-pretty it's actually beautiful I like funny-macabre
A wicker casket, for example What's good? No, literally, what is

"good"? You say *good looking* or *good writing* or *True Detective*
I don't understand the proxy convo you're having couched in

"aesthetics" I can't even hear the cicadas over the sound of yr
judgment Listen, I don't want to be Trojan Horsed or nothin

but yr taste is too canonical to me "Control" by Janet Jackson
is one of the greatest songs in the nation Warm hearts sparkle

in the colonial afternoon Control is a reaction to something
smacking that cracks the future w/ no precedent We call this a

paradigm shift—say we were totally blindsided Janet wants to
take control from her parents From the loss of a first love

Control of the narrative Janet wants to Black Cat in boxy
military garb Janet wants to show you her midriff and intro-

duce J.Lo to the general public in a few albums and yeah, have
her tits out at the Super (Bowl) in a minute Shock is a kind of

collision A booming confusion The shudder and the shot are
almost indistinguishable Shock has its electric correlate, but is

also itself by what surrounds the event: a quiet dinner party
vs sweaty racing thoughts And what do you make of it My

friend said he found out his crush graduated college in 2014 n
hates himself And I'm like wait til yr my age, thinkin *I totally*

still look like I'm in my 20s Then it turns out the dude you were
makin out with was born the year *Janet*, the album, came out

What the literal fudge An hour ago you were singing "That's
the Way Love Goes" at karaoke In my defense, taller dudes

always look older How to negotiate control and the lack of
control When yr slap hand gets itchy OK whenever anybody

dumps you, just think of them as if a gif of a white dude wilding
out to Wu-Tang in a cardigan then suddenly falling into the

Grand Canyon—Dating is all the way dumb I don't know what,
if any of this, will reach yr peepers but I want to ask you this

(and I am guilty of making ppl wade thru some bullshit b4
getting to my point): what do you turn to when breath dashes

from yr body like it's on the lamb? Cindy Crawford says lighting
is everything Take a selfie from the sunblown window Even

supermodels say "lighting" It's comforting! But there's also
value in exposing yr engine #BadSelfie Archaic but also so

fresh: self-expression Trust is a thing that guides you thru a
feed The voice like a handshake I'm in front of you There is

paper and a trade-off This is ancient, like pixel drift What's
under the hood of irritation We call complication a knot A

knotted life that doesn't get to be undone Who here has a clear,
linear rope? Denial! You have to love yr knots You have 2 shout

them out Curate if need be Janet turns her knots into songs
Sonic beauty (tho fuck beauty) Knot is the response A man-

ager is like a politician Not the minutiae but the orchestration
The dark forest It's hard not to inhale The cave is where to

turn when you've no other recourse This isn't a discussion This
isn't a mandate (lol man date) This isn't an answer This is a

lineage: Lascaux, Keith Haring, Rihanna How do you draw
breath? In and down Heel to crown Janet says I'm in control n

ends Don't make me lose it As if she knows what's to come
The battle of control is in learning to make, and giving it up

This is not abt being the "good" one—that's boring This is abt
the wrong one, the petty one, the ugly one, the gruff one, Ruff

and Threadbare White waves caught in a loop from microphone
to loudspeaker Returning output to input What's yr feedback?

Plz spoon it to me as if it's my business Does it vibrate like
Paula Abdul bumpin in a Janet video? Does it make sense? Can

we just agree—Fuck sense Do you see the blades in the field Do
you see the crust of walnut cream cheese on my crush Do you

see the goopy eyes flash across his face when he finally "sees"
me *It's good to lead with something pastoral, it's more universal*

that way A person is always inserting I don't believe in "uni-
versal" b/c ppl r always like *gravitas* and *sacrosanct* and

pastoral and yesterday Science said We've conducted a study
and think medicinal smoke may eliminate certain airborne

bacteria Look Science, NDNs have smudged for thousands of
years Why do you always think *you* bring the truth? Curate yr

Junk to allow for a close-up I'm aces 2 b spontaneous just give
me time to fix my face first Pretty Little Lyres Bite guard on a

nightstand Insomnia is like hearing cicadas but the cicadas are
yr brain and yr brain is an egg being smashed by time after

time *Dummy, once yr not arranging yr Junk to control my inter-
pretation—you're becoming So Becoming* I want you balls deep

inside me Occupied is a throaty valve of relief filling the room
I'll make a supersonic manatee out of you UGH so many Junk

words wading in imprecision and then suddenly a weapon Like
"family values" Niqui says "*Values?* What does that even mean?"

But also *family* What I'm tussling with is the pathway from
definition to validity *Dummy, is this the poem or the essay abt*

the poem Pennies fall out of my crotch when I stand up Clap!
Laugh! Must have slipped out of my coin purse when I took the

change from brunch It's like a diorama of class anxiety What
goes into the display case vs What goes into the Junk drawer

Things that make me want to run: (1) Seeing other ppl run (2)
Eatin a whole pizza (3) Everyone adoring the same person *Prove*

it says every actor who's ever been in a police procedural Do
you ever call yr booty "Incorrigible" in the sense that it refuses

to quit? Boner overwhelms the ability to think, says every Hart
Crane poem The journalist at the Moby-Dick exhibit asks

What's your white whale? And I says to her I says *Dick, just like*
in the book lol Flight Fight Feed Fuck says my cute, reptilian

brain Relief in the Sense of context: 5 milligrams + 50 dollars =
100 percent sure of Sleep, then 80 > 85 > 50 > 15 percent

What a hypnic jerk The body can acclimate to anything I repeat
Pebble Bubble Fountain three times in the mirror Reading the

news used to make me feel more knowledgeable and in that
way more aware and in that way more powerful Now I just

want to dye (my hair) Flaming asteroid for president 2016 plz
Tinder Grindr Jack'd Scruff OkCupid Adam4Adam Squirt

Surge Manhunt The operative phrase is "dumped" but the opera-
tive feeling isn't "garbage" bc garbage suggests refusal and I

can be reused I swear All the comments fall in ringlets, like
comets I was going to say Streak but then thought about skid

marks and demurred I stare and shake in the static which is like
a magic eye autostereogram that doesn't become a turtle or a

saxophone or whatever Until a kind of instinct to re-ho (as in *to become a ho again*) kicks in *Hey are you Teebs* and immediately

I ask *Is this a summons* I never think I do anything wrong but
people cuss at me from cars *No* he says *I'm yr date* Classic case

of someone not looking like their profile pic Oh enough with
slimy love I can't wait to read all of *your* breakup tweets All of

your divorce status updates and Instagram calls to respect yr
privacy Your love is about as relevant as chewed gum under

the table I just flipped *I got too drunk to sleep it off* says Aca-
demia on the language of Academia The first charming thing

you said to me was that when you walk behind a woman at
night you walk slower farther away so she doesn't think yr

tryin to run up on her Even do something gay like laugh in that
helio high balloon laugh you laugh How can you claim to respect

life if you don't also care abt yr enemy If you call them enemy
must be something worthy of yr grace Harry Potter pops into

the discussion strangely as it shd for adults It's strange to
occupy without investment, to selectively remember, like me

with Harry Potter or most forms of popular culture for that
matter Or like u and NDNs on Thanksgiving Every year I'm

surprised that genocide is an excuse to unfurl America's shame-
less gorging As if gorging isn't going off whole hog every other

day tbqh *Some stuff happened n it's an occasion for me to stuff
my face,* is also a thing I say at a Hunger Games movie Of what

concern is permanence to the poem I let myself Skittle ballpark
nacho Junior Mint Sour Patch Kid buttery fluff n tumble kaleid-

oscope-like aswirl on the insides The world finally quiets What
concern is permanence to the poem Giving up candy makes

"one" a boring moron I'm just spitballing here You've a whole
entire sunset behind yr fingernails I've prayed to every goddess

for a fat ass but if my backside is to be believed: I have no
messiah Meet me in the dogs I'm always in the process of being

dumped but also by my own fantastic imagination which I've
been calling my imag-mag Carbon butt print Zan works w/ this

waiter he calls TGI Fridays bc of his wide Chiclet smile & dead
eyes *Lol she says she's a top* I think TGI Fridays wants to fuck

me? Blooming onion appletini Yum yum yum mini donuts My
body is accumulating toxins and feelings Coffee, for example, is

convenient pain My bff says poets are the stewards of language
and being a stew-stew of lang-lang, I came up with a new word:

sleeding, which is the body sleeping & bleeding I mean there's
hearts on my pillow Literally I got a tattoo last night, on my

shoulder of hearts It scabbed over There's beer, in general An
air of smoke traces the air Sleek finish gel to stiffin yr hair Cake

batter buttercream goops up my skin I want to smell like what
I eat Gimme brains A phone is *I* beaming into my brain TV is a

screen into the thing I call: phone, heart, brain *I googled you in
the rain* I see you on the street cross to avoid me We look at

our phones I mean pain Is the disgust at hearing yr own voice
or face in the true mirror or body in the video recording—is that

a body rejecting itself Cute guy on the train looking away or the
shop girl saying *You can't leave yr zine here* The shudder post-

rejection is a Junky primordial tether *Passing wind* is the
most hilarious phrase in America I've been using the word

aromatic to refer to ideas that unfold like wine I'm at Shake
Shack with Andrew bc cheese fries r the spell of our generation

and I'm lookin to conjure Adele rings the air while singin Purity
is so fascist Everyone is going on a juice cleanse rn I dew love

a diet Quitting is the best feeling The gentle thrill of hooky I
HAVE A JUNKY DIET I swallow all the colors of our omnivorous

rainbow More accurately: I am Kumeyaay As such part of me is
confrontation and part of me (in) denial This is what I call

survival A bulgy dude presses fingertips to hips in front of me
Rocks to and fro Some ppl just need to be told *No* more often

I'm in every gay love triangle in Brooklyn: I like You, You like
Him, He likes Me: I like tall guys, You prefer blonds, He's a leg

man We die by the hilt of our turn-ons But the sword tips Just
the tip Who can you talk to the way you talk to yr therapist I'm

not going to just turn down a donut unless sex in the derriere is
comin Everywhere smells like sweaty parmesan and no one

seems bothered but me People often overlook the gravity of the
Erykah Badu lyric, "I'm feelin kinda heavy/cos my high is comin

down" Watchin someone return to their phone with the attn of
a new crush makes me pissed as a port-o-potty Sad Slut Sorry

for Stealing Sixty Cent Stamps from the Post Office this Snowy
Sunday I have no investment in yr sizable manhood except it

looks so good catching moonlight, then my mouth The bananas
are dying and this is not a metaphor Cheaply made is synony-

mous with vulnerable to disease, in agricultural terms Homo-
geneity breeds blind spots Commercially produced yellow

penis proxies are clones and share the same backdoors How
do you slip into a banana You have to start before it's born

What peach doesn't love flesh How long can you keep it 2gether
It falls away It falls away it falls nm too healthy Watermelon

gummies harden in the open air You expect me to tie bananas
into the narrative I expected my Ancestors wd b treated as

human beings Janet says *Let's wait awhile* Coil and release
Anger is another biting thing A smooth seething But seductive

for its clarity, like pain Writer Ppl say We're post narrative, post
characters, post enthusiasm, post structure, post connection,

post meaning I too have the internet She introduces plants to
Janet Jackson Post Postal Post-It Post up Poster Post huh The

scroll is both pre and post page Pages are kind of quaint, no?
Unspool as if a runway on which I walked in the thrift shop At

the time, there were three main industries on the rez (besides,
of course, meth): fire dept, RV park, and the thrift shop Mom

worked at each of them I spent whole ass afternoons among
the busted watches and raggedy Barbies n rolling green candy

bowls Sugar was first cultivated in India the trade became a
major colonial industry I'd parade in faded dress and sweaty

plastic pumps Candy is a simple way 2 make kids behave when
you have three jobs Appetite is explained by simple biology

"Sorry for the genes" is a phrase mom is often fond of saying
You literally can't argue with Gobstoppers Auntie calmly blinks

"That's just your way" The dispossessed are denied history
Them hidden things aggregate, like saccharides Thrift shop

smell, to a young fairy formatting normalcy, is basic Not in the
sense of boring but Elemental A thing yr composed of n comp-

osing A face in the mirror makin mirror-face Have you ever
wondered why thrift stores always smell the same? The musk

settles like a dusty comfort feeling Feel the tide of decision swell
in and roll out, never quite catching it It's defeating, so much

older than I was 15 yrs ago & for a breakup to feel like the first
one Is this time travel? My tolerance is cry baby I would very

much like it Very much beg u dunk yr front Junk into my back
Junk Sober daytime sex is the nakedest It was hotter then Our

bodies aromatic as cracked something Everyone, you said,
knows their number unless it changes Like losing oodles of

weight or suddenly becoming middle class When things change
hands, their designation depends on intent A riding crop, for

example It's easy 2 overlook a mass's deviations n particulars
from the outside I'm saying: strain (in general [to pasta]) The

taste is basic but the mouth feel like a mushroom of foam bed
I finally get haiku Simplicity that exposes its breast bone, the

more uncompounded Tho as Junk I'm less an element n more
the entire periodic table I'm from a place where ppl became

garbage A pile to remove Junk is an upgrade Poverty is like this:
you keep everything until the wheels fall off and then you eat

the wheels I go dull in the dull blast of words Let's address this
now: being broke is not the same as being poor Poverty is a

trauma It sticks Mangled like a long thin silver chain in the Junk
drawer I sort of loved digging you/up Figuring out how to

make a sad person laugh is my daily task, so I enjoyed the chall-
enge Do you ever walk around & randomly remember what a

good experience I had at the DMV four years ago or just me?
Don't try me dummy, I'm not in the mood The Kelly Clarkson

song called "Einstein" with the chorus "dumb plus dumb equals
you" *Nope* Love in the Time of Cholas *Fine* The sadness act-

ivated isn't where I wanna rest How sad to only feel suspicious
love Subcutaneous suspicion or sometimes thorny suspicion

Ossified suspicion Hedwig's journey thru "Wig in a Box," finding
a way through the perceived prison of makeup and wigs into

Identity Haven't figured out how to be NDN and not have
suspicion coursing thru me like cortisol But we all have our

struggles I'm learning to be less weary of abstraction It looks
periwinkle Sorry my mom's a synesthete I've had to suffer

through so much abstraction in these book things You can at
least give me a few more pages *Hunger is a room to be tended* is

the kind of sentence I resent In fact, if you don't like everything
I like you're a goddamned dog pornographer Abstraction how

can I say this, my rancor isn't anti-intellectual I just hate it when
you never use contractions Do you wanna do something fun?

Do you wanna say *larp* five times fast? Larp x5 The Berdache
The Shaman The Noble Savage The Indian Problem The Squaw

The Indian Princess The Spirit Animal The Drunk Indian The
Teary-Eyed Environmentalist Considering something as a gen-

eral quality or characteristic apart from concrete realities,
specific objects, or actual instances From the Latin word for

separation *Work it like yr workin a pole* God I can't believe I'm
actually going to write this: Hi I like myself It's taken me seven

generations to dig my Junk situation It's how I'm seen, felt, and
fought The American imposition that rumbles my coffee break

I shout into the god The god buffers In the buff Shit, that
Erykah lyric is actually "feelin kind *hungry*/cos my high is

comin down" Speakin of Munchies *It's okay to be wrong, dummy*
My squishy delicious brain begs me to write but the couch in

the office siren-songs like rich vanilla in almonds, *Nap gentle*
hero, Nap damn you From the window, the city grows brickish

beanstalks tall and fat and largely dark Only a craptacular
society would build luxury rooms not even the lights will live

in while so so many sleep in slumps surrounded by all their
Junk What's the material significance of an empty luxury

apartment What's it like to express potential over utility Are
not lost on me The sky in snowflakes humping a big turquoise

Eames chair on the street The featureless Upper East Side The
hard up city El Niño year had me thinkin snow might not even

happen The kitchen junk the closet junk The shoes I always
mean to resole If Junk is the space in between utility: the poet in

writer's block And somehow the Junk, aka History, aka Snow
keeps piling up There are far too many beauties who think

they're trash too many dipshits who think they're god's gift
Too often impaled by the reflex to ascribe meaning onto *things*

The movie stub for example I miss your very adult body In my
neighborhood, in the bars I go to, nobody has an adult body

Ppl talk about cartoons and have faces that slide shut as patio
doors when I say *what's up* Some things reach w/o trying, like

a bartender with dimples In the morning he rolls over *You shd*
get going if you want to catch yr bus on time UGH don't break

the moment with yr shirking derp yolo internetese Or future
tenses (*what if we . . .*) or catastrophic personal narratives abt

the kind of guy you *can't* be Once, a generation was a gener-
ation Now even just a few years' gap it's like I'm an eld n then

have trouble sliding into sleep Plz let's stay Buoyed by pillows
by knees I double back onto u Send yr nerves shooting like a

mind understanding new terms *So what do you do?* Is a thing
ppl ask at parties n bars n the morning after dark sex in New

York Whenever I'm back in CA my whole rez asks *Soooooo*
what r you doing? Which means, *what's more important than*

being here w/ yr family and yr ppl in the valley we've lived in for
thousands of years Which, heavy I have ppl out here too Make

here feel like *home* Sucks bein a sometimes person Sometimes
here sometimes there The mind like arthritis But really I'm

lucky Some ppl never get ppl Some ppl make them up Get
locked up for talking to them I've never been locked up but I

did come out as bisexual & was afraid of my own voice once
for 28 years But now, karaoke And the whole block knows

when I stub my toe It sounds like this: UUUUUUGGGGGHHH
Sometimes I hear my voice back n wonder if I even went thru

puberty Junk is a come up for ppl treated like garbage of the
state More mass shootings this year than there are days in a

year Men in Texas surround a mosque Erect their open carry
law in time for my trip to Austin I can't remember the last time

I was so skittish Except when I saw that drone in the city The
eerie sputter of the world shifting Or just about anytime I use

the toaster Blimpy eyes trained on the bread slits Possessions
possess A park bench overlooking the backlit skyline of the

city's trunk Powerless, dark, deafened and more stars over
Faggotland than we'll ever see again Sandy alarms all around

us but I'm warm in yr arms Winter is a season of accumulation
I have layers, like an onion is the stupidest online dating profile

"about me" I've read in a minute Men are a waste of attention
You can lead a man to Beyoncé, but you can't make him think

Let's get anti-romantic Let's get disgusting My kink is holding
hands on the way to the deli I hate musicals so gd much *Not*

every revelation deserves a stanza, dummy The hope is unity
The reality a bit more sandpapery Refurbish The hands are

welding torches The clear tube-light the torch smirks outward
The cutting edge The *tink tink* of paper clips A clear pink plastic

swordfish tiki drink stirrer America is all action, no memory
Me, mostly memory and laughing at the proposed stripper

name "Diphtheria" America wants its NDNs weary, slumped
over the broken horse, spear sliding into the dry grass But I'm

giving u NDN joy NDN laughter NDN freedom My body was built
for singing The notes drive my mottled sky Catch them one by

one Trill at will Wizard the A's and D's C's and such in piles on
the staff, clef, etc I'm worried self-love will make me lazy *No*

dummy, it's yr natural state The Kumeyaay custom of burning
the dead's possessions, ascending the objects to heaven, was

a lot simpler when everything was organic Junk smoked w/o
the spirit infuser A note isn't useful until you sing it Store them

in yr ear *Didn't quite hit the note That wasn't such a good time*
American "Freedom" is such historical propaganda Indigenous

and black lives remind American exceptionalism that slavery,
theft, and genocide are its founding institutions Buy me a donut

and take me to a museum Reach for my hand or the spot on my
neck when it rained and we ran the ten sloppy blocks back to

my place—Bring me a cool bowl of sherbet when I get high The
base forming rings on the thigh of my jeans My brow forming

beads on yr shoulder America is like, *I'm just trying to get my
happy back* America is like, *but I'm a good person* Never the

body of its atrocities Never the Chinese Exclusion Act Never
Jim Crow Never the Indian Removal Act Never the Japanese

internment camps Just because you don't know about them
doesn't mean they go away Who built the railroads Who picks

the crops Who delivers yr egg bagel on a rainy day Our tower is
missing bricks Fingers to lips it's a wonder we make anything

I'm a tenant of suspicion Did u know in Chile, *pico* is slang for
penis? I'd always just thought of beaks like in pico de gallo but

a pecker's a pecker And then that fabulous round thing, "lang-
uage," taps me on the back and I fall over A. R. Ammons is like,

I have this feeling to write a poem but it was a boner Oppression
is the wages of comfort We walk down 14th Street and you see

14th Street but I see a massacre Lenape land An unfortunate
side effect of living is the world doesn't care What a way 2 stay

stoked: Pepper objects with life and ride or die To ascribe
victimhood to Junk is to miss the point completely There's a

calm outside the anxiety of utility There's a freedom from use
for the sake of use An affection for just *being*, a new kind of

worth outside of the object Perhaps I've lost my grip I saw my
ex or like the body of him not the face Or, the hairline not the

pomade The shoulders but not the cape Yet for a couple mean
seconds he was somehow 2,760.4 miles from NYC Somehow in

front of me in line at this coffee shop in downtown San Diego
ordering a maple bar and iced coffee I froze n literally buckled

It's never just abt the night in question My body holding onto u
despite myself or bc of it America is all action, no memory Me,

mostly memory and farting on airplanes Pull down the orange
ex-boyfriend box behind the Container Store plastic storage

drawers on top of the Expedit IKEA bookshelf Swing states
Under appreciated patience Straight dudes painting their nails

Asking of a main character, is this a normal person in extra-
ordinary circumstances, or an extraordinary person Can u be

ambitious w/o being anxious I'm in the moment I'm in the
moment I'm in the moment A metal chair screeching on con-

crete Bridgegate The base of the former World Trade Center
turned into a Westfield Shoppingtown Faggotland is extra

digital these days A registry that tracks queers' location—
what's the danger in that? A torso shot or the Williamsburg

Bridge A gruff couple words (hot, you looking?) Then a pin
drop Do you really expect me, sight unseen, to come over to

yr (murder) apartment Buzz up like takeout n ask "Who
ordered the ass?" I'm not sex negative I'm just weary of a

culture of explosions It's never just the night in question
Thumbing into plastic wrapped grocery store ground beef *Let*

him go like the bright yellow socks w/ blue toes Auntie sent last
winter, dummy Brackish I mean bratty My mind wardens I'm

sorry I'm sorry I'm sorry *Stop apologizing, dummy* How long do
you hold on to childhood survival strategies Like a sponge but

for feelings More armored in the new years But growin up on a
rez gripped by meth it seemed like anything could catalyze

violence Auntie cackling one minute then accusing u of givin
her “that” “look” Yelling at you until you cry Uncle Cookie

shooting his rifles at night Threat flows thru my valley I used to
hide in there, like my ancestors There’s too much world Still I

try to see it Look, I’ll compromise: I won’t get the cookie dough
brownie bites frozen yogurt n beloved chili cheese corn snack

Fritos But I’m scarfing the banana chips, dried mango n cacao
nibs Baker’s chocolate sucks Anything coffee flavored that isn’t

coffee is an abomination Buttered popcorn flavored jelly beans
are literally the next extinction level event Many ppl can be in

their bodies w/o moving all the time Baffling I’ve snail-trailed
all over this Anything still is in danger *Dancing in moonlight, I*

know you are free Run in a zigzag Part the part I didn’t get the
part The middle part (it was the 90s) I wd go down on Chris

Pratt tho All my friends are BOTS—Babes of the Struggle The
mind is so much fire and bull Get some marshmallows How do

we protect ourselves from car commercials and the border
patrol Mom and Amber hands behind their heads facedown

on the asphalt at the checkpoint There is something sick abt
accusing an NDN of bein an illegal immigrant And something

sick about the phrase "border patrol," and "illegal immigrant"
like white ppl where was *your* green card when the sun never

set Seeing as how borders r erected in part to pen in the poor
Plenty money jumps over under in & out borders as a matter

of course This is my heroic, sweeping sentiment This is my red
love The pinch of sun floating thru the blackout curtains in the

old apt on South 8th in a sharp disbelief our two rivers met
downstream A mirror fell the day I discovered I was living my

future n for the first time in my adult life experienced a
moment of happiness arm in arm w/ security All my little faces

are smiling Life, I look forward to living you completely, with
all my shattered selves All divisions of reflection All the ppl

who ppl like us are required to be Touch is the first step of dis-
carding Some things, seen simply Simply need to leave A niche

ecology Large, breaking, beautiful time This gallery owner hits
on me by telling me he's a gallery owner He spent all day in his

gallery I say *Lucky gallery having you shoved inside it all day* w/
a straight face Like a common thot A Land Before Shame Some-

times life's a "call is coming from inside the house" situation
and That Ho Over There is really The Ho Within I still have a

few skies left to rise toward A few other giant Earths to un-
earth A few (hundred) (more) clippings to collect Slapping

noises *Look at you dummy, adding proxies of yrself onto the
world & reaffirmed by them* Yr rip currents r proof that it's still

possible to get lost inside you Do significant swells write them-
selves When I started this I was delirious frenetic and in the

cyclone I found Teebs, the bratty diva, my alter ego *You rang?*
I put him on and everyone loves him He is piss & vinegar &

libido & punchlines Everyone wants to chat w/ him, desper-
ation and all He's onstage, a whip He cracks and cracks up He

doesn't "do" hesitation Just hyperbole I wear him on dates
and he always gets a text on the way home I wear him under

the red lights He's a flashbulb All the men say so *Fuck yeahhhh*
says Seattle, corner of his lip curls upward *That's it baby take*

it all Oh my God So does Baltimore & DC & Philly & Portland &
Boston & Northampton & Providence They all want to fuck

Teebs and after a while I forget that he comes off But the more
I AM Teebs the less I'm writing because writing requires the

hesitation, the fear, the insecurity, the reflection So Teebs I'm
going to leave you in the lines I can write you or I can be you

but not both Touching all yr Junk hides it from obscurity Not
wanting to feel absence because absence is a grief In her book,

Kondo suggests going thru yr Junk one item at a time, holding
the various *its* and asking *does this spark joy* Point being: the

Little Mermaid made me a packrat The whittling process A
training program in settling back into yr miracle What remains

criminally un-let-go-of Don't worry abt Junk It literally doesn't
worry abt you It can't *Excuse me? I was here on the first date I*

*am the pin slid thru the boutonniere I am the b&w strip of photo
booth first kiss I am the small stuffed leopard you held all the*

*way thru the Natural History museum Your time wd mean
nothing without me* Nostalgia is the original second life It might

as well be a construct Living on an imagined construct over
the course of these pages I can understand how someone could

sustain faith in something (divinity) that literally doesn't exist
And how less real is this *I am the polaroid of just before you*

*pulled his pants down to the b&w tiled bathroom floor at the
album release party I am the pack of matches from the third*

date first fuck when u thought Trophy Bar, remember this *I am the pumpkin tote bag you won together at Halloween trivia*

night, after the tie-breaking walk-off to "Nasty" by Janet Jackson I am I am I am Let's blow this popsicle stand So the popsicle

stand leaned its head back and sighed like a house settling and undid its pants The fight made a possibility of us ending

descend Summer shifting uncovered a fault line *September 11 made us afraid* But I'm from an NDN reservation, raised that

way The rest was aftershocks You pulling slowly away Pay (attention [to me]) The pleasure of lifting yr shoulders Sit

down and push yr soles into the ground *I'm the plane ticket bookmark Jet Blue Portland 2014 trip I'm the business card from*

the New York Times *reporter on yr flight to Bogotá I'm the flyer for the zine benefit show when you worked the merch table and*

gave him a handy behind the bar Running into the poem like cold waves in our fat Far Rockaways n thrash til homeostatic

Waves create a craving for Dr Pepper Somethin sweet to cut the salty somersaults and deft kelp evasion and hrs n hrs

coaxing friends farther in, but they never want to go as far out as us do they? Past the point of wave-beaten Past the point of

even being subject to waves Where the huddled ocean cups
you and blows, like soup Smooth pie crust like a desert island

Shots of expensive silver tequila reminiscent of beach sand
The proven psychological tide of butter Spectral dynamics n

guitar riffs Ambulance sirens Pretty much any guy over 6'2
who all eventually say *move on* Especially with tattoo pain and

nerve death before a root canal or calls from the rez A note to
say someone else is in the hospital or passed on Sudden 98

degree days Dash out to meet yr gentleman jetty n forget to
signal on the freeway The SUV next to you crashes into the

divider and rolls and you had summer school with him But to a
lesser extent, how abt kneelin close to shore or sitting down in

small sharp waves The breakers fill yr mouth like salty choco-
lates *They said we wouldn't last, we had to prove them wrong*

Suddenly we're not 2gether 4ever It's been almost 2 months
since I looked across a table in Union Square Park w/ the city

beginning, reluctantly, 2 shed its summer skin Low key pee
smell The table an odd bright green You started as a character

in a poem It felt sly, meeting you that first time, and only a little
silly falling into a ditch I mean a word that rhymes with *glove*

Almost two cranberry months since I said what you expected
Lychee martini Popping a boner in the ocean Sunscreen smell

on the morning sheets I wd be lying if I said I missed u Or that
I made the wrong choice I'm not sure I ever gloved you It was

wrong of me to say it To build a monolith of expectation They
called the club in Orlando "Pulse" bc the walls, painted white,

would pulse with whatever color the lights were that night
Imagine the splattered white walls In the silence that followed,

the only noise was cellphones Desperate family and friends
wailing praying against their bottomless suspicion It's all I cd

think about that day You were a sanctuary for my grief The
words felt easy bobbing down the river of my voice A human

shaped mate of devastation A tether I may have believed my
glove for you was real but only really for that day All night I

watch headlights sweep across your ceiling The empire rises
Conspiring The sky is moody The land is not much better The

news is not looking good IT's NOT lookiNg Good Brexit Le Pen
Duterte Putin The reasons to be afraid accumulate I'm thinkin

of a claw foot bathtub and cracked wallpaper in a scary movie
trailer A paper doll dress in the black vacuum of space Casually

google what wd happen to a body without a space suit Cold is
the currency of the universe Warm is the outlier, folks Deep

freeze in the ongoing bleak Beings of a pumping heart that, like
everything, goes cold How cd I not be obsessed with hugging

the core of this world and fisting engines of light Making fire
and swaddling ourselves in skins I don't always use the most

vigorous verbs But I did go on a date tonight where at the end
we got frisky and he said (fingers on the seam of my ass crack)

that he actually has a boyfriend and they're not open He just
still likes going on dates Dates! Literally the worst part of a

romantic enterprise Cold starship boldly blasting into new
lands and new civilizations powered by a crystal of the imag-

ination Abstract infused by an image and a refusal to explain
a fuel source No wonder they were post money in *TNG*

Wherever we go, needs feed and I find it harder and harder to
believe benevolence is the thing Thousands of Yazidi girls

missing and plastic fills the ocean's mouth and the cursive of
yr name still occupies the canopy of my throat Fuel, the under-

pinning What fires your gd engine Rigor, mortis Cold as
unmoving or unmoved The opposite of music Warm in the

cold universe Molten, forming A rock becoming magma
becoming lava becoming land Land, the trauma of lava Lava

the lamp of the ancestors and later a cheeky find in the Junk
shop and rising in our living room Living groom Just bc nothin

cares doesn't mean it lacks *meaning* What is the point of
curiosity but a train rolling past the spot where the Donner

party feasted n then go on a four hour Wikipedia downward
spiral I'm the closest thing to a mime parade I whisper, home

late tiptoeing down the creaky hallway tryin not to wake my
roommates Nice chicken parm, sluts, I say to my fingers at

lunch Dissociation is evacuating from the inside *I just know
we'll have a good time* Junk: a relief map of yr traumas Dipping

yr whole arm into the bin of sunflower seeds I'm in my Shonda
Rhimes *Year of Yes* and so far it's pretty freak Gave a beej to a

logger in town for a football game at his hostel Almost wrote
hostile The old-fashioned way, as in I met him at a bar after

lingering eye contact No apps Told him I was writing this poem
Flush with success after only eating half the cheeseburger for

dinner For the first time in my life it wasn't no burger or four
burgers Full on Rocky situation He said he was flattered every

time his gf's gay friends grabbed his beer can Bacon-wrapped-
date flavored Doritos The artifice of order Predictability,

measured time, present wrapping Order, Order, Pockets of
Order Or, Durham I dumped a boy from Raleigh today The

baton of Junk The dance whirls Whorls War Tortle So what if I
doggy-paddled into the ocean to crap Whales shit in the ocean

all the time Cut to mall dressing room thousand outfits mon-
tage Ignorance as a tool to revive the feeling of doing somethin

new Junk has 2 b the poem of our time Pointless accumulation
Clinging to a million denials Why do you need an assault rifle?

What if radioactive bears Buying in bulk Afraid of forgetting
that party in 2007 when Chantal shouted JAMIROQUAI IS

HOLDING THIS PARTY TOGETHER!!!! Junk is the garbage ppl
keep Didn't they tell you I'm a meteorologist but for people

What's that called? Psychic? Psychic side chick In maths,
"arbitrary" is a thing without specific value Quite the Junkery

The world, all of its rock formations and space missions and
presidents and religious phobias and fashions fossils All of it

has always seemed so arbitrary to me, bc to survive this long
into an occupation feels sometimes so arbitrary to be And

then sometimes so divine Who else cd survive but my line It's
true, your Junk won't save you from a tsunami, but I'm desc-

ended from a group whose culture history language gods
cosmology calendar stories government gait was capital O

Obliterated I'll stop writing this when it stops happening So
when I "get" anything it's hard to let go Resisting death for

generations, I want to make the opposite of death No excuse
for a vanilla bean tapioca ball attitude Ever bought a McFlurry

n shouted YR DEAD INSIDE but yew were pointing a finger at
yrself and, horrified, yew screamed Ran home but halfway

home yew forgot what yew were doing and bought a pair of
sneaker boots at DSW or just me? That's what I thought Could

this be flip The whole body of it Could this mean nothing Have I
led you out here just to leave you howling at the moon What

I'm trying to say is this is a poem of vibrant inconsequence
Picture it: Sicily, 1923 Whoops I mean Thanksgiving dinner w/

family in town from the rez at a midtown resto, blackberries
in the whipped cream while the Washington Redskins blaze on

TV behind us Or last month when police clashed with water
protectors Tore down encampments and elders and children

On the same day milk-toned Oregonian militiamen r acquitted
after armed occupation of land On the same day the Cleveland

Indians r in the World Series during American Indian Heritage
Month Before, in the past, this world discovered war Berlin

Afghanistan Terracotta Slob War War War on the front of every
newspaper In the back of every noggin Sludgy nympho gummy

bear humps the Haribo package—Body monuments and light
cigarettes Diet Cherry Dr Pepper and a bag of Hot Cheetos

Cholera epidemic in Haiti where there is no immunity because
Cholera was like the only thing that never befell Hispaniola

Rasp is sassy but Junk is punk Static in its intention Static in
its emotional release Static in the city Buzz of disbelief White-

house domes every convo *We are a part of the rhythm nation* I
get this teaching gig and being an authority figure, let me tell u,

is such an emperor-has-no-clothes situation Like being onstage
Very, "I'm more afraid of you than you are of me" Sharon Jones

glides on about being an injured prison guard on Rikers Island
Terry Gross asks, "How were you able to convince the prisoners

that you were strong enough and focused enough to do the job
and keep them in line?" Sharon says "It's the look in my eyes . . .

You could not show fear, and that's one thing I didn't show" Try
it on Saying "*pilfer* is a fun word" enough times makes it true,

like petticoat coffee cakes and the invention of blue raspberry
Dummy, stay on message I never intended to be a professional

NDN but this time of year every1 wants to know do I celebrate
Thanksgiving? Janet is still with us, despite the retreat of

common sense, the retreat of fall, the retreat of Sharon Jones
and David Bowie and Prince and Vanity and Leonard Cohen

Phife Dawg and George Michael Do you remember what it was
like to feel warmth from the sun? It's odd, right? For light to

only be light and not also heat The sun conceals things too, in
its glare There's nothing but me and you in this book even tho

sometimes I have B.O. and my credit card gets stolen and I
need a new pair of gloves It makes sense that it took me the

whole year before I could entertain talking to u again Back in
our crystalline season I was right 2 suspect worth in yr grace

You aren't evil for not loving me Maybe it's a retrograde sitch
Look into the sky in yearning to be someplace else When you

gobble gobble so fast it's like dinner never happened & even
now conjuring you feels like a diversion but yr the reason I

started writing this in the first place Michelle Tea says when
you write about someone, you have to be able to look them in

the face Your faces are many Your shoulders are different
colors Sometimes yr EXTREMELY tall and sometimes only very

tall Sometimes yr face is golden smooth and cut like an English
garden Sometimes yr face is lunar, bright chalk white n

cratered Sometimes we were together for six weeks Sometimes
eight months Sometimes I don't know yet We sit still in our

gurgle sacks waiting for each other to change Waiting for our
stomachs 2 glow pink again in the gallery night But we dimmed

Each time we dimmed differently but we dimmed we did The
Metro Link light rail SEPTA MTBA Amtrak Bolt Bus Megabus

the Peter Pan the MAX Metro North MARC Train Charm City
Circulator The opposite of escape A firming in the firmament

The couch An airbed Yoga mat and sometimes just the floor I
just want to close a door I'm masturbating in the bathroom like

a common teen Man punches woman at bar Man screams at
woman in diner Man yells at woman in a hijab in Queens "Man,

man, menace" is like a weird game of "duck, duck, goose" The
hollow taste on the inside of yr mouth when you haven't eaten

all day Make out with boys named Patrick n Gerald n Martin n
David and suck on his finger at the bar with the empty blue fish

tank and rando lotto ball cage Drink Shiners in his backyard
Threesomes are awkward af mostly bc everyone is wasted so

it feels like heavy turbulence on the twin bed in this liver I
mean sliver of apartment Double stuffed and hating it Last

Resort Lagunitas Goose Island The shot special Two more
packages of Reese's Old-Fashioned Narragansett and Jameson

on the rocks Whatever insulates you from the calving face of
this gd world When has sympathy for the oppressor ever

worked for us? The poem and reading the poem become each
other Echolocation The sound of a shape Fog is a dopey meta-

phor The news leaps through me like a talking dog—unreal,
no? I don't know where the feeling is or what to do with it n

spent most of the day w/ my eyes squeezed shut but then I
went for a run to force feed myself some endorphins Wrote a

few couplets and texted all my friends and went to the rally
and marched bc it felt restorative to blast night with my voice

box and stomp the sidewalks and the streets with friends for
twenty blocks in all directions Whole blocks of avenues in all

directions swell w/ peeps shouting MUSLIM RIGHTS ARE
HUMAN RIGHTS and MY BODY MY CHOICE and BLACK LIVES

MATTER and WATER IS LIFE and TRANS LIVES MATTER and
PUSSY GRABS BACK and then we got a drink and for a couple

hours it seemed like we'd just been in some horrible dream
As if the fog lifted and we could hear thru the static Feel the

sun again But it's only growing colder This is just the beginning
And the path back from complacency is lion mane I was afraid a

long time before these days We talk about Athena Farrokhzad
and palimpsest and what can you *even* believe We talk about

illness in *Don't Let Me Be Lonely* and a sudden awareness of our
fingertips We talk abt the Origin of "Obligation" Latin *obligatus*

meaning "bound" and the stem *obligate* which in biology means
an organism restricted to a particular condition of life Which

originates in the Latin ob + ligatus, past participle *ligare* which
means to tie or to bind Ligate in English to tie up as if in surgery

The agent a ligature which in typography means when 2 letters
are tied into a single character like a & e to æ or & which is the

Latin e + t which in Latin means "and" like in *et al* or *et cetera,*
etcetera Which, ligatures and abbreviations, have been around

since the innovation of the written word bc time is money and
the earliest forms of writing were 4 accounting as in how much

grain in yr silo or yr pyramid if yr a historical revisionist *There are times when I look above and beyond* Dissociation: thank you

for keeping me sane and alive when when when I needed you
Smell of warm bread baking in the 5AM But now I'm looking to

connect & inhabit more than I want 2 slip away Crunchy chocolate granola Cliff bars Staring at our fingernails I'm building the

archive of a life that shouldn't exist, while it still does Bathroom
bills Running into the drummer ex-boyfriend with his guitarist

bf and they get yr name wrong Wristband from that gay club in
Cartagena where we danced w/ the self-proclaimed Perez Hilton

of Colombia Every bar frankly should have tostones smellin up
the grill Having made out with the server at the vegan resto @ a

Tuesday gay karaoke night Is a poem about Junk itself merely
an accumulation of doomsday and birth certificates If part of

Junk is letting go, partly Junk is letting go of you Junk finds a
new boo I am the standard of my mind Smoke pulls back

into the fire and the fire pulls back into the Junk and the Junk
pulls up to the bumper, baby We lie quiet in the buff, not touchin